COUNTERAIR
OPERATIONS

Air Force Doctrine Document 3-01
1 October 2008

Interim Change 2 (Last Review), 1 November 2011

This document complements related discussion found in Joint Publication 3-01, *Countering Air and Missile Threats*

SUMMARY OF CHANGES

The Air Force Doctrine Working Group has reviewed this document and recommended that it remains valid and will again be reviewed no later than April 2013. AFDD numbering has also been changed to correspond with the joint doctrine publication numbering architecture. AFDD titles and content remain unchanged until they are updated in the next full revision. The cover to AFDD 3-01, *Counterair Operations* has been updated to reflect revised AFI 10-1301, *Air Force Doctrine* (9 August 2010), information. A margin bar indicates newly revised material.

Old Number	New Number	Title
AFDD 2-1	changed to AFDD 3-1	*Air Warfare*
AFDD 2-1.1	changed to AFDD 3-01	Counterair Operations
AFDD 2-1.2	changed to AFDD 3-70	Strategic Attack
AFDD 2-1.3	changed to AFDD 3-03	Counterland Operations
AFDD 2-1.4	changed to AFDD 3-04	Countersea Operations
AFDD 2-1.6	changed to AFDD 3-50	Personnel Recovery Operations
AFDD 2-1.7	changed to AFDD 3-52	Airspace Control
AFDD 2-1.8	changed to AFDD 3-40	Counter-CBRN
AFDD 2-1.9	changed to AFDD 3-60	Targeting
AFDD 2-10	changed to AFDD 3-27	Homeland Operations
AFDD 2-12	changed to AFDD 3-72	Nuclear Operations
AFDD 2-2	changed to AFDD 3-14	Space Operations
AFDD 2-2.1	changed to AFDD 3-14.1	Counterspace Operations
AFDD 2-3	changed to AFDD 3-24	Irregular Warfare
AFDD 2-3.1	changed to AFDD 3-22	Foreign Internal Defense
AFDD 2-4	changed to AFDD 4-0	Combat Support
AFDD 2-4.1	changed to AFDD 3-10	Force Protection
AFDD 2-4.2	changed to AFDD 4-02	Health Services
AFDD 2-4.4	changed to AFDD 4-11	Bases, Infrastructure... [Rescinded]
AFDD 2-4.5	changed to AFDD 1-04	Legal Support
AFDD 2-5	changed to AFDD 3-13	Information Operations
AFDD 2-5.1	changed to AFDD 3-13.1	Electronic Warfare
AFDD 2-5.3	changed to AFDD 3-61	Public Affairs Operations
AFDD 2-6	changed to AFDD 3-17	Air Mobility Operations
AFDD 2-7	changed to AFDD 3-05	Special Operations
AFDD 2-8	changed to AFDD 6-0	Command and Control
AFDD 2-9	changed to AFDD 2-0	ISR Operations
AFDD 2-9.1	changed to AFDD 3-59	Weather Operations

Supersedes: AFDD 2-1.1, 26 April 2002
OPR: LeMay Center/DD
Certified by: LeMay Center/DD
Pages: 52
Accessibility: Available on the e-publishing website at www.e-publishing.af.mil for
    downloading
Releasability: There are no releasability restrictions on this publication
Approved by: LeMay Center/CC, Maj Gen Thomas K. Andersen, USAF
    Commander, LeMay Center for Doctrine Development and Education

FOREWORD

The mission of the United States Air Force is to fly, fight, and win in air, space, and cyberspace. A crucial part of achieving that mission involves obtaining and maintaining superiority in the air domain. That domain, defined for the first time in this publication, is the area, beginning at the Earth's surface, where the atmosphere has a major effect on the movement, maneuver, and employment of joint forces. Within that domain, forces exercise degrees of control or levels of influence, characterized as parity, superiority, or supremacy. The US has enjoyed at least air superiority in all conflicts since the Korean War. The US will probably retain that superiority in today's ongoing conflicts, but the prospect of near-peer competitors in the not-too-distant future raise the possibility of air parity – a condition in the air battle in which one force does not have air superiority over others – or even conceding superiority to the adversary if Air Force forces are not properly employed.

Our possession of air superiority helps enable joint forces to dominate adversary operations in all domains and to achieve a wide range of cross-domain effects. Unless we can freely maneuver in the air while denying the enemy the ability to do the same, we do not have superiority. Therefore, this publication addresses how the commander of Air Force forces can best employ his assets within a joint force to achieve control in the air domain to enable the overall joint force effort.

Counterair is more than just force protection or air and missile defense. It also includes offensive actions against an enemy's capabilities, allowing us to seize the initiative and force the adversary into a defensive posture. Furthermore, counterair is executed by more than just air assets. Counterair is a joint, multinational, and interagency team effort, comprising a combination of command and control systems, intelligence, surveillance, and reconnaissance systems, aircraft and missile systems in air-to-air and air-to-ground roles, and surface-to-air defense weapons.

The effect of air superiority is not normally an end unto itself. Air superiority provides enormous military advantages, allowing the joint force greater freedom of action to carry out its assigned missions (freedom to attack) while minimizing its vulnerability to enemy detection and attack (freedom from attack). The success of any major air, land, or maritime operation may depend on the degree of air superiority achieved. This Air Force doctrine document provides guidance for designing, planning, integrating, coordinating, executing, and assessing counterair operations. It provides operational doctrine to gain and maintain control of the air. As such, it focuses on how air forces can be organized and employed to successfully conduct counterair operations.

STEPHEN J. MILLER
Major General, USAF
Commander, LeMay Center for
Doctrine Development and Education

TABLE OF CONTENTS

INTRODUCTION

PURPOSE

This Air Force doctrine document (AFDD) establishes doctrinal guidance for counterair operations and supports basic Air Force doctrine.

APPLICATION

This AFDD applies to the Total Force: all Air Force military and civilian personnel, including regular, Air Force Reserve, and Air National Guard units and members. Unless specifically stated otherwise, Air Force doctrine applies across the range of military operations.

The doctrine in this document is authoritative, but not directive. Therefore, commanders need to consider the contents of this AFDD and the particular situation when accomplishing their missions. Airmen should read it, discuss it, and practice it.

SCOPE

Counterair operations may be necessary throughout the range of military operations. These operations run the gamut from the defense of the North American continent to striving for air supremacy in a major theater war, to enforcing a no-fly zone in a peacekeeping operation, to passive defensive measures in a humanitarian relief operation.

FOUNDATIONAL DOCTRINE STATEMENTS

✪ The air domain is the area, beginning at the Earth's surface, where the atmosphere has a major effect on the movement, maneuver, and employment of joint forces. (Page 1)

✪ Control of the air is normally one of the first priorities of the joint force.

✪ Counterair is a mission that integrates offensive and defensive operations to obtain and maintain a desired degree of air superiority. (Page 1)

✪ Counterair helps ensure freedom to maneuver, freedom to attack, and freedom from attack. (Page 1)

✪ Air control describes a level of influence in the air domain relative to that of an adversary, and is characterized as parity, superiority, or supremacy. (Page 2)

✪ Air superiority is that degree of dominance in the air battle of one force over another that permits the conduct of operations by the former and its related land, sea, air, and space forces at a given time and place without prohibitive interference by the opposing force. (Page 3)

✪ The objective of offensive counterair is to destroy, disrupt, or degrade enemy air capabilities by engaging them as close to their source as possible, ideally before they are launched against friendly forces. (Page 5)

✪ The objective of defensive counterair is to protect friendly forces and vital interests from enemy airborne attacks and is synonymous with air defense. (Page 6)

✪ Air refueling is an essential enabler of counterair operations. (Page 6)

✪ Effective integration of intelligence, surveillance, and reconnaissance assets is often as crucial to successful counterair operations as are traditional lethal effects. (Page 6)

✪ The joint force air and space component commander's first priority should be to define—in both time and space—that level of air control needed to achieve the joint force commander's objectives. (Page 21)

✪ To prevent fratricide, great caution should be exercised when employing autonomous combat identification in defensive counterair operations. (Page 27)

CHAPTER ONE

COUNTERAIR FUNDAMENTALS

We must be prepared to control the air above the Earth's surface or to be buried beneath it.

**—General Charles Horner,
Combined force air component commander
during Operations DESERT SHIELD and
DESERT STORM**

The US Air Force flies, fights, and wins in the domains of air, space, and cyberspace. This publication concerns control of the air. Control of the air provides the joint force with freedom of action while reducing vulnerability to enemy detection, attack, and other effects. Joint doctrine provides broad guidance for countering air and missile threats (see Joint Publication [JP] 3-01, *Countering Air and Missile Threats*), but does not describe the full spectrum of air control, as this publication does. The Air Force brings specific capabilities to a joint force to achieve various levels of air control by operating in the air domain. Clearly defined domains help identify the conditions and capabilities under which systems and personnel conduct operations, but do not mandate or imply command relationships. **The air domain is the area, beginning at the Earth's surface, where the atmosphere has a major effect on the movement, maneuver, and employment of joint forces.**

Control of the air is normally one of the first priorities of the joint force. This is especially so whenever the enemy is capable of threatening friendly forces from the air or inhibiting a joint force commander's (JFC's) ability to conduct operations. **Counterair is a mission that integrates offensive and defensive operations to attain and maintain a desired degree of air superiority** (JP 1-02) Counterair missions are designed to destroy or negate enemy aircraft and missiles, both before and after launch. **Counterair helps ensure freedom to maneuver, freedom to attack, and freedom from attack.**

Counterair is directed at enemy forces and other target sets that directly (e.g., aircraft, surface-to-air missiles) or indirectly (e.g., airfields, fuel, command and control facilities, network links) challenge control of the air. Airmen integrate capabilities from all components to conduct intensive and continuous counterair operations aimed at gaining varying degrees of air control at the time and place of their choosing.

> *"The first task of airpower is to gain and maintain air superiority. Air superiority is essential to air, ground, and sea operations"*
>
> **—General William W. Momyer, Commander, 7th Air Force and Military Assistance Command Vietnam Deputy Commander for Air, 1966-68**

COUNTERAIR OPERATIONS

Counterair operations are conducted across all domains and determine the level or degree of *air control*. **Air control describes a level of influence in the air domain relative to that of an adversary, and is categorized as parity, superiority, or supremacy**. The level of air control can range from a parity (or neutral) situation, where neither adversary can claim control over the other, to local superiority in a specific area, to supremacy over an entire operational area. Levels of control may vary over time. (Figure 1-1 illustrates their relationship.) US forces enjoy air superiority or supremacy in today's ongoing operations,. Air superiority is often required to enable the successful execution of joint operations such as strategic attack, interdiction, and close air support.

Normally, counterair operations are classified as offensive or defensive. However, airpower's inherent flexibility allows missions and aircraft to shift from defensive to offensive (or vice versa) to adapt to changing conditions in the operational environment. Counterair operations can be conducted across the tactical, operational, and strategic levels of war by any component of the joint force. Operations are conducted over and in enemy, friendly, and neutral territory. They range from seeking out and destroying the enemy's ability to conduct airborne attacks with both aircraft and missiles, to taking measures to minimize the effectiveness of those attacks. The JFC's objectives and desired effects determine when, where, and how these operations are conducted to gain the desired degree of air control.

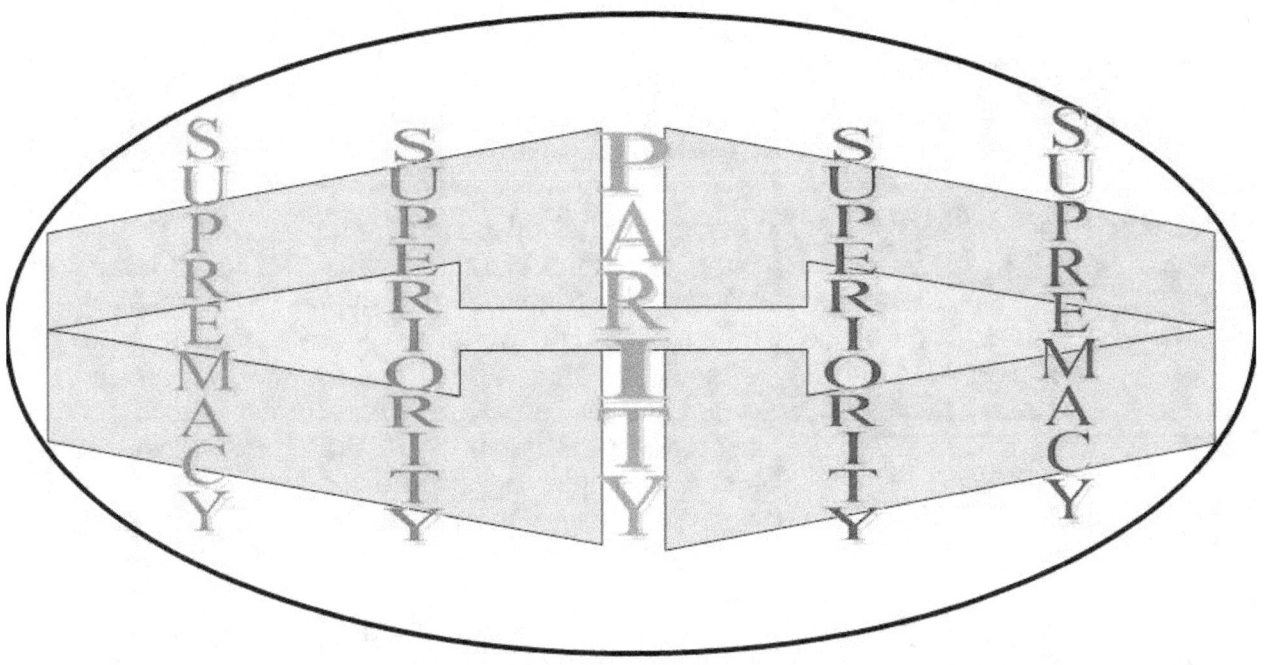

Figure 1.1. Air Control Relationships

⊙ **Air parity.** A condition in the air battle in which one force does not have air superiority over others. This represents a situation in which both friendly and adversary land, maritime, and air operations may encounter significant interference by the opposing air force. Parity is not a "standoff," nor does it mean aerial maneuver has halted. On the contrary, parity is typified by fleeting, intensely contested battles at critical points during an operation with maximum effort exerted between combatants in their attempt to achieve some level of favorable control.

⊙ **Air superiority. That degree of dominance in the air battle of one force over another that permits the conduct of operations by the former and its related land, sea, air, and space forces at a given time and place without *prohibitive* interference by the opposing force** (JP 1-02). Air superiority may be localized in time and space, or it may be broad and enduring.

⊙ **Air supremacy.** That degree of dominance in the air battle of one force over another that permits the conduct of operations by the former and its related land, sea, air, and space forces at a given time and place without *effective* interference by the opposing force. Air supremacy may be localized in time and space, or it may be broad and enduring. This is normally the highest level of air control to which air forces can aspire.

So What Is...Parity, Superiority, or Supremacy?
It Depends...

In modern warfare, parity is often not recognized at the moment it exists. It is more easily identified when viewed in a historical context as the point in time just prior to when momentum swung to favor one combat force over another. During the 1973 Arab-Israeli War, in the Sinai desert Egyptian surface-to-air missile (SAM) batteries were employed so effectively that the Israeli Air Force—an otherwise extremely effective force—could not accomplish its mission with traditional tactics of air interdiction or suppression of enemy air defenses, even though the Egyptian air force was similarly unable to interfere with Israeli maneuver.

Both air and ground force maneuvering essentially came to a halt for a 48 hour period. The stalemate—the period of air parity—was not broken until the Israelis changed tactics by using direct infantry attacks on the Egyptian SAM system, an example of integrating capabilities of the full joint force into counterair operations. Those attacks swung the momentum back to the Israeli side by allowing their Air Force to regain control of the air domain, and eventually assert air superiority across the entire front.

By war's end, the Israeli Air Force was virtually unchallenged in the sky, and had therefore established air supremacy.

—Various Sources

The concept of air superiority hinges on the idea of preventing *prohibitive* interference to joint forces from enemy air forces, which would prevent joint forces from creating their desired effects. Air supremacy prevents *effective* interference, which does not mean that *no* interference exists, but that any attempted interference can be easily countered or should be so negligible as to have little or no effect on operations. While air supremacy is most desirable, it may not be operationally feasible. Air superiority, even local or mission-specific air superiority, may provide sufficient freedom

of action to create desired effects. Therefore, commanders should determine the minimum level of air control required to accomplish their mission and assign an appropriate level of effort to achieve it.

The continuing proliferation of weapons of mass destruction (WMD) increases the importance of air superiority. Several nations have advanced air-to-surface and surface-to-surface missiles capable of delivering WMD. In addition, the electronic warfare capabilities of some potential adversaries have advanced to near parity with the US, which may enable aircraft capable of delivering WMD to penetrate friendly air defenses. Mobile missiles, cruise missiles, and unmanned aircraft systems (UAS) pose a significant threat to friendly forces and populations, and the ability to locate and destroy these systems prior to launch remains a challenge for effective counterair operations. These threats may have larger implications – for example, the survival of diplomatic relationships, political alliances, and even civilian populations may hinge upon successful countering of a missile threat.

Offensive Counterair (OCA)

The objective of OCA is to destroy, disrupt, or degrade enemy air capabilities by engaging them as close to their source as possible, ideally before they are launched against friendly forces. Otherwise, OCA operations seek out and destroy these targets as close to their launch locations as possible. These operations may range throughout enemy, friendly, and neutral territory and are generally conducted at the initiative of friendly forces. OCA includes targeting enemy air defense systems, airfields and supporting infrastructure; theater missiles; ground, sea, and air based launch platforms and supporting infrastructure; command and control, communications, cyberspace, and intelligence nodes. OCA operations enable friendly use of contested airspace and reduce the threat of airborne attacks against friendly forces.

Defensive Counterair (DCA)

The objective of DCA is to protect friendly forces and vital interests from enemy airborne attacks and is synonymous with air defense. DCA consists of active and passive air defense operations including all defensive measures designed to destroy attacking enemy airborne threats or to nullify or reduce the effectiveness of such threats should they escape destruction. The basic active defense criteria to detect, identify, intercept, and destroy remain the same for any airborne threat. DCA forces generally react to the initiative of the enemy and are subject to the weapons control procedures of the area air defense commander (AADC). For further information on the AADC, see JP 3-01.

AIR REFUELING REQUIREMENTS

Air refueling is an essential enabler of counterair operations. Many air assets that perform the counterair mission have relatively short on-station times or operate from bases far removed from their intended targets. These assets rely on air refueling to extend range, on-station time, and tactical flexibility. Strategists and planners should build needed refueling support into the air component's planning products. Refueling coordination also requires constant management by planners. Detailed refueling instructions should be included in the air tasking order (ATO) SPINS and the air control order (ACO).

For details concerning air refueling operations, see Air Force Doctrine Document (AFDD) 2-6, *Air Mobility Operations*.

INTELLIGENCE, SURVEILLANCE, AND RECONNAISSANCE (ISR) REQUIREMENTS

Effective counterair operations require timely, reliable, and accurate intelligence, so proper joint intelligence preparation of the operational environment (JIPOE) can be crucial to counterair operations. Near-real time information from air, surface, and space-based sensors may provide warning, situational awareness, targeting, and assessment. ISR is also needed to identify and attack or exploit emerging targets that pose a substantial threat to friendly operations. Timely target detection, development, and geolocation, as well as weapon selection, mission planning, and assessment all depend on integrated collection and analysis. **Effective integration of ISR assets is often as crucial to successful counterair operations as are traditional lethal effects.**

Without an accurate, well-defined enemy air order of battle (AOB), friendly forces will operate under increased risk. JIPOE may provide important clues concerning *how* an adversary may use his own counterair capability—for instance, how he is trained and what doctrine he uses. Further, while JIPOE cannot provide predictive analysis or read the mind of the enemy commander, it can provide valuable clues as to the enemy commander's intent. Other component intelligence resources can provide valuable information concerning air operations within their areas of operations.

The ISR and strategy divisions within the air and space operations center (AOC) determine and prioritize the air and space component's collection requirements, in order to develop measures and indicators used to assess counterair operations. These measures and indicators help evaluate whether friendly actions have been accomplished and desired counterair effects within the operational environment have been created.

For further details systems and requirements, see AFDD 2-9, *Intelligence, Surveillance, and Reconnaissance Operations*.

CHAPTER TWO

ORGANIZATION AND COMMAND AND CONTROL (C2)

> *The flexibility of an air force is indeed one of its dominant characteristics.... Given centralized control of air forces, this flexibility brings with it an immense power of concentration which is unequaled in any other form of warfare.*
>
> **—Air Chief Marshal Sir Arthur Tedder**

Effective counterair operations require a reliable C2 capability. C2 assets should be capable of exchanging information rapidly with other Services, components, and multinational partners. The information flow supports the chain of command and should be as complete, secure, and near real time as possible.

Centralized control and decentralized execution remain a fundamental tenet of airpower; advances in technology have not changed this. C2 systems are tailored to support this tenet. Centralized control is exercised from the appropriate command level while permitting decentralized execution of counterair operations. Decentralized execution means that the lowest echelon possible is given responsibility for determination of mission requirements and achievement of mission success. The capabilities of modern communication and real-time display technologies, however, make centralized execution—such as direct control of missions from outside the cockpit—possible. During several recent operations, senior commanders have attempted a degree of control approaching centralized execution. *Such command arrangements may not be effective in a fully stressed, dynamic combat environment and so are seldom, if ever, appropriate for counterair operations—especially OCA.* The loss of situational awareness and tactical flexibility entailed by centralized execution of counterair missions may often degrade mission effectiveness. For greater detail on centralized control and decentralized execution, see AFDD 1, *Air Force Basic Doctrine*, AFDD 2, *Operations and Organization*, and AFDD 2-8, *Command and Control*.

The six months of major combat in Operation ENDURING FREEDOM in Afghanistan saw not only centralized planning, but also a degree of centralized execution that was unique in the US experience… [Technology] allowed sensor-to-shooter links to be shortened, in some cases, from hours to minutes. It also, however, resulted in an oversubscribed target-approval process that lengthened rather than compressed the kill chain. As a result, the human factor became the main constraint impeding more effective time-critical targeting…

This unprecedentedly [sic] close connectivity, however, cut both ways. Although it was helpful—and even essential—up to a point, it also often resulted in gridlock, in that it encouraged higher-level leaders and their staffs to try to micromanage the fighting. Senior leaders often intervened at the tactical level not because circumstances required it, but simply because they could. As a result, fast-moving targets sometimes were allowed to get away.

Another consequence of our expanded global connectivity was that 'reach-back,' a desirable capability when used with discrimination, metamorphosed into 'reach-forward' as rear headquarters sought information from US Central Command's forward-deployed combined air and space operations center (CAOC) and then used that information to try to influence events from the rear….

—Benjamin S. Lambeth
by permission, excerpted from *Air Power Against Terror:*
America's Conduct of Operation ENDURING FREEDOM

Nonetheless, the nature of global communication in this day and age virtually guarantees a degree of political sensitivity and operational visibility completely alien to the generation of Airmen who fought before the US involvement in Vietnam. Air Force forces cannot expect to operate in a completely unconstrained environment. Rules of engagement (ROE) are *"directives issued by competent military authority which delineate the circumstances and limitations under which United States forces initiate and/or continue combat engagement with other forces encountered"* (JP 1-02, *Department of Defense Dictionary of Military Terms*). Effective operations require the establishment and promulgation of easily understood ROE. ROE are established to convey the intent and guidance of national leadership and senior military commanders with respect to the use of force. They reflect political imperatives that may impact the operation's overall end state and may thus place restrictions on use of force, engagement authority, etc. ROE and special instructions constrain (compel) and restrain (prohibit) certain military actions. Though restrictive, these measures do not constitute centralized execution.

Observations from OEF:

...the [Predator] images also caused headaches for the commander of regular US forces in Afghanistan who was overseeing the operation. Throughout the battles in the Shah-i-Kot region, command personnel at higher levels, and operating in other locations, relayed numerous questions and much advice to the commander in the field in an attempt to contribute to the management of unfolding battle.

...the episode reveals the powerful influence that live pictures from the battle zone can have on the ability of the on-site commander to determine and execute a successful battle plan. The last thing the US field commanders need is an over-complicated chain of command, with officers thousands of miles away from the scene of battle providing armchair advice on the basis of pictures rolling across a television screen.

— **Anthony H. Cordesman,** ***The Lessons of Afghanistan: War Fighting, Intelligence, and Force Transformation***

Centralized execution may lengthen the friendly decision cycle and the dynamic targeting process (the "kill chain"), but the sensitivity of certain end state conditions may require C2 arrangements that approach centralized execution in rare cases. When this happens, operations should revert to centralized control and decentralized execution as soon as practicable. Refer to AFDD 2-8, *Command and Control*, for details.

There has been a tendency for ROE to become more restrictive as the level of hostilities has diminished in the concluding phases of most recent conflicts. This tendency can result in ROE that, in effect, drive operational plans toward centralized execution. Such "overly centralized" ROE are contrary to the natural function of air forces. They can lead to a collective mindset whereby Airmen begin to rely on ever-increasing levels of oversight and approval, and eventually become dependent on them to execute. As such, commanders should be careful not to create ROE so restrictive that they place friendly forces at unnecessary risk or at an operational disadvantage.

In any case, while restrictive ROE may exist, centralized execution of counterair operations is much rarer than in the conduct of other operations such as strategic attack or nuclear operations. For example, during Operation SOUTHERN WATCH, there were many restrictions on use of deadly force against Iraqi air defense facilities, but there was very little interference in how individual missions were flown in support of the operation. Airmen at the tactical level had the latitude to execute in a decentralized manner.

COMMAND RELATIONSHIPS

Airmen should expect most counterair operations to be joint and combined efforts. Therefore, it is essential that Airmen understand the counterair capabilities of other components of the joint force and how to integrate those capabilities with those of the Air Force. The commander, Air Force forces (COMAFFOR) normally exercises his command function of Air Force component forces through the AOC. The JFC normally designates the COMAFFOR as the joint force air and space component commander (JFACC, or combined force air and space component commander [CFACC] in the case of combined operations). In this case, the AOC will become the core of the joint (or combined) air and space operations center (JAOC or CAOC). For the rest of this publication, it will be assumed that the COMAFFOR is also the JFACC.

Although assets capable of performing counterair missions are assigned to different components, the JFACC is normally the supported commander for counterair operations. The JFACC's responsibilities normally include planning, coordination, allocation, and tasking based on the JFC's priorities and guidance. Additional responsibilities include air defense, airspace control, and ISR efforts. As such, the JFACC is normally appointed the roles of AADC and airspace control authority (ACA). Assigning responsibility and authority to coordinate and integrate airspace control and counterair operations to one air commander greatly enhances the effort to gain and maintain control of the air.

For more on the integration of airspace control and air defense operations, see AFDD 2-1.7 *Airspace Control in the Combat Zone*. A more detailed description of command relationships for counterair can be found in AFDD 2 and JP 3-01.

Area Air Defense Commander. The AADC is responsible for integrating the entire (air, maritime, and land based) air defense effort and should be the component commander with the C2 capability to plan, execute, and assess integrated air defense operations with other air operations. Splitting the assets among multiple commanders reduces their effectiveness. Any attempt to separate missile defense from the overall air defense structure has the potential to seriously degrade the overall air defense effort and increases the risk of fratricide among multi-layered air defense assets. The AADC is also the engagement authority for air defense operations and normally will not delegate that authority below the regional or sector air defense commander (RADC or SADC) or the theater air control system (TACS) control and reporting center (CRC). (See below for an explanation of these elements of the TACS.) For further details, see Air Force Tactics, Techniques, and Procedures (Inter-Service) (AFTTI[I] 3-2.17, *Theater Air-Ground System (TAGS)*.

With the support of the Service or functional component commanders, the AADC develops, integrates, and distributes the area air defense plan (AADP). This plan should be closely integrated with the airspace control plan (ACP). Planners should strive to create a reliable and consistent common operational picture (COP) (i.e., a fused and correlated air, ground, maritime, space, and cyberspace picture) available to all supporting C2 facilities. The AADP should arrange a layered, overlapping defense to allow for multiple engagement opportunities, contain detailed weapons control and engagement procedures, and specify airspace control measures (ACM). More detailed descriptions of the AADP and the ACP are available in AFTTP[I] 3-2.31, *Integrated Air Defense System (IADS)*.

One of the most critical responsibilities of the AADC is to provide guidance and articulate procedures for combat identification (CID). CID is defined in JP 3-09.3, *Joint Tactics, Techniques, and Procedures* (TTP) *for Close Air Support*, as "the process of attaining an accurate characterization of detected objects to the extent that high confidence and timely application of military options and weapons resources can occur." AFDD 2-1.9, *Targeting*, depicts three levels of CID. The first level identifies the track or entity as friendly, foe, or neutral. The second level identifies platform type, while the third level attempts to determine the target's intent. Accurate and timely identification enhances real-time tactical decisions by allowing timely, beyond-visual-range engagement of enemy aircraft and missiles while conserving resources and reducing the risk to friendly forces. CID information may be obtained from various land-, air-, and space-based systems, along with ACM documented in the ACP or the ACO. To be most effective, this CID "system of systems" requires effective guidance from the AADC and a common data link backbone with the goal of seamless near-real-time information sharing among platforms. To avoid a single point of failure, no one node acts as an exclusive conduit of all CID information. Electronic methods, which provide the most rapid and reliable means of identification, are normally used when available. Visual and procedural means of identification are not as practical but may be required in some situations. Some individual weapons systems retain an autonomous CID capability. For details on CID, see AFTTP(I) 3-2.31.

Airspace Control Authority. The ACA is responsible for airspace control and for coordinating the use of the airspace. Normally, the JFC will designate the JFACC as the ACA. The ACA develops policies and procedures for airspace control and for the coordination required among components within the theater. The ACA establishes an airspace control system for the JFC, integrates that system with host nations, and coordinates user requirements. The ACA develops these procedures into an ACP and, after JFC approval, promulgates it throughout the theater. The ACP is then implemented through the ACO. The ACO is an order that provides the details of the approved requests for ACM. While the ACP provides general guidance for control of the airspace, the ACO implements specific control procedures for established time periods. It is published either as part of the air tasking order (ATO) or as a separate document. The ACO may include ACMs and fire support coordinating measures such as air routes, base boundaries, and restricted operations areas. A key responsibility of the ACA is to provide the flexibility needed within the airspace control system to rapidly employ forces.

AIRSPACE CONTROL

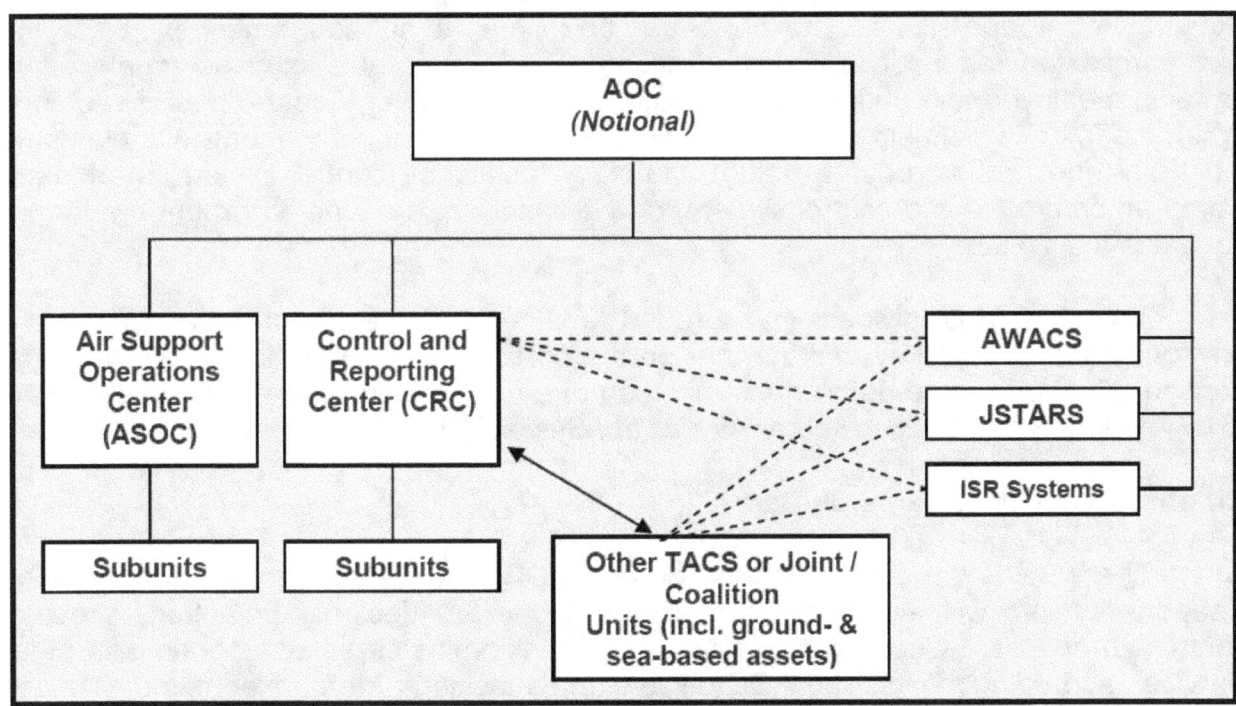

Figure 2.1. *Notional* **C2 Arrangement for Airspace Control**

The JFC establishes the geographic boundaries within which airspace control is to be exercised and also provides priorities and restrictions regarding use of the airspace. Airspace control is normally one of the primary functions of the Air Force TACS. Figure 2.1 depicts several major elements of the TACS involved in airspace control and shows how they interrelate. The TACS is structured to conduct airspace control, OCA and DCA operations, and other air operations. A secondary function of the TACS is to minimize the risk of harm to friendly forces. Since different Service components have operational control (OPCON) of specific counterair assets, the C2 structure is designed to integrate with other components to provide responsive and timely support. For more on theater airspace control, see AFDD 2-1.7, *Airspace Control in the Combat Zone*. See also AFTTP(I) 3-2.17 for details concerning other components' contributions to joint theater air C2.

COMMAND AND CONTROL RESOURCES AND REQUIREMENTS

The COMAFFOR uses the following C2 resources to conduct and support counterair operations:

Theater Air Control System

The TACS provides the COMAFFOR with an overarching means of commanding and controlling counterair operations. It includes the personnel, procedures, and equipment, such as the AOC, necessary to plan, direct, control, and assess air operations and to coordinate those operations with other components. It is composed of units and communications nodes to allow centralized control and decentralized execution of air operations. The TACS can be tailored to support contingencies of any size across the range of military operations. TACS elements may be employed in garrison, deployed for contingencies, or deployed to augment theater-specific systems. When the TACS is combined with other Service or functional components' C2 elements (such as the Army air-ground system, the Navy tactical air control system, the Marine Corps air command and control system, or the special operations air ground system) it becomes the TAGS.

The TACS is divided into ground and airborne elements, based on the environment in which they operate, not on the portion of the operations for which they provide C2. For a more detailed examination of each element of the TACS, see AFDD 2-1.7, AFTTP 3-1, Vol. 26, *Theater Air Control System*, and AFTTP(I) 3-2.17..

Air and Space Operations Center

The AOC is the senior element of the TACS and is the principal air operations weapons system with which combat air operations are designed, planned, directed, controlled, and assessed. Additionally, the AOC coordinates air operations with other Services and components. The AOC disseminates tasking orders, executes day-to-day peacetime and combat air, space, and cyberspace operations, provides rapid reaction to immediate situations by exercising positive control of friendly forces, and provides the capability to conduct dynamic targeting, including the prosecution of time-sensitive targets. When the COMAFFOR is appointed J/CFACC, then the AOC becomes the core of the J/CAOC. Within the AOC, the airspace control management team integrates the use of airspace in the theater. It provides the current air and surface situation using data from many sources and is responsible to the ACA for developing airspace control procedures through the ACP and coordinating airspace control activities. The AOC ensures that the ACP is compatible with current operational requirements and capabilities and relies on the ACP to ensure missions are de-conflicted.

The AOC may perform certain airspace management and airspace control functions directly, or may delegate them to the control and reporting center (CRC) or other tactical C2 agencies. Among the roles that the AOC may perform directly include data link management among all components and participating nations (vital for CID and air battle management) as well as management of the overall air defense effort. It may also perform C2 liaison, mission control, combat search and rescue (CSAR) assistance, threat warning, and coordination of air defense artillery and friendly artillery fire if it does not delegate these functions to the CRC or other tactical C2 elements.

TACS Ground Elements

Control and Reporting Center

As part of the TACS ground element, the CRC is the airspace control and surveillance radar facility directly subordinate to the AOC. It provides theater mission control through employment of C2 elements of the TACS. The CRC is assigned an airspace control sector by the AOC. It manages and directs activities of all deployed Air Force surface radars within that sector.

The CRC's primary mission is to provide airspace management and airspace control, including air traffic detection, tracking, and identification. The CRC also issues scramble or airborne orders; performs some data link management functions, and manages air defense activities within its sector. Additionally, the CRC provides C2 liaison, mission control, navigational assistance to CSAR efforts, aircraft threat warning, and coordination with air defense artillery fire direction centers and the friendly artillery warning service, although in some cases, these functions may be performed directly by the AOC. The CRC may further delegate control of surveillance areas to subordinate radar units or airborne warning and control system (AWACS) aircraft within its sector for optimum radar and radio coverage and air battle management.

Within the TACS, the CRC communicates up to the AOC, down to subordinate units, and laterally to other TACS/joint/coalition units to ensure defensive assets are employed in mutually supporting roles within its assigned sector. The CRC battle staff directs fighter aircraft, air defense artillery, and other counterair assets. The CRC battle commander, acting as a RADC or SADC, normally establishes operating procedures for initial assignment of airborne targets to air defense artillery and fighters. All air defense elements coordinate continuously with air defense artillery fire coordination units to eliminate duplication of efforts and ensure adequate commitment of assigned weapons against threats. Execution authority for air defensive systems may be provided to the CRC as part of the RADC/SADC responsibilities. Given a constrained CID environment, the CRC may be the lowest tactical level that possesses engagement authority for enemy air threats.

Air Support Operations Center (ASOC)

As part of the TACS ground element, the ASOC is the functional air component responsible for planning, coordinating, controlling, and executing air operations that directly support ground combat forces. The ASOC can affect the counterair battle through coordination for suppression of enemy air defense (SEAD) missions, management of some airspace control measures, and others. The ASOC is usually collocated with the senior Army tactical echelon and coordinates operations with the permanently assigned tactical air control party, Army fires cell, and the AOC.

TACS Airborne Elements

Airborne Warning and Control System

The AWACS provides the TACS with a flexible and capable airborne radar platform. It provides an initial battle management function as well as command and control capability and is normally among the first systems to arrive in theater during contingency operations. Through voice and data connectivity, AWACS issues air defense warning, directs aircraft on counterair missions, manages air refueling, provides an air picture to air defense forces, assists with navigation, and coordinates CSAR efforts. AWACS can detect and identify hostile airborne and surface-to-air missile (SAM) threats and assign weapon systems to engage enemy targets.

AWACS may carry an airborne battle staff or airborne command element (ACE) authorized to redirect forces under the authority of the JFACC. When employed with an ACE, AWACS can scramble and divert aircraft conducting counterair operations and recommend changes in air defense warning conditions. The AWACS can perform many, but not all, CRC functions.

Joint Surveillance Target Attack Radar System (JSTARS)

The JSTARS is a long-range, airborne sensor system that provides real-time radar surveillance information on moving and stationary surface targets via secure data links to air and surface commanders. JSTARS can play an important role in the effort to gain control of the air. When combined with other ISR sensors, JSTARS contributes to the commander's overall situational awareness by identifying and locating such targets as SAM missiles, launchers, and radars and antiaircraft artillery (AAA) sites, among others. The system has expanded into an integral part of the TACS. JSTARS provides updates on enemy force disposition and performs limited battle management functions, which may be important in managing the OCA effort. JSTARS information builds situational awareness for the JFC and JFACC to manage air operations, to update target information, and to provide real-time dynamic targeting.

**AWACS, JSTARS, and RIVET JOINT provide C2
and ISR information to the TACS and other users**

ISR Systems

Although not specifically part of the TACS, spaced-based and airborne ISR systems (both manned and UAS) are key enablers of counterair operations, (e.g., SEAD). For example, RIVET JOINT (an airborne signals intelligence collection and reporting platform) can provide near-real-time assessment of hostile airborne, land, and sea-based electronic emitters via secure communications directly to the AOC and the cockpit of aircraft conducting OCA operations. In addition, the U-2, MQ-1 (Predator), MQ-9 (Reaper) and RQ-4 (Global Hawk) provide near-real-time streaming video and still images of enemy air defense systems (e.g., SAM sites) to help determine status for attacking OCA assets and may, in the case of some armed UAS platforms, perform direct attack OCA missions.

CHAPTER THREE

COUNTERAIR PLANNING, EXECUTION, AND ASSESSMENT

THE COUNTERAIR FRAMEWORK

Offense is the essence of air power.

— **General H. H. 'Hap' Arnold, US Army Air Force**

Like other air, space, and cyberspace operations, counterair is fundamentally effects based. This means that counterair operations are designed, planned, executed, assessed, and adapted in order to influence or change system behavior to achieve desired outcomes (AFDD 2) Effective counterair operations should be part of a larger, coherent plan that logically ties the overall operation's end state to all objectives and effects and tasks. This plan should guide execution and the means of gaining feedback and measuring success must be planned for and evaluated throughout and after execution. This approach should consider all potential instruments of power and all available means to achieve desired effects, and must consider the entire operational environment. The operational environment is a composite of the conditions, circumstances, and influences that affect the employment of capabilities and bear on the decisions of the commander (JP 1-02). Non-military instruments of national power may not seem relevant to counterair operations, but they can be decisively important in certain circumstances, as when diplomatic efforts permit or deny basing or overflight rights that critically impact counterair efforts. Conversely, counterair capability can help deter hostile adversary action by providing a credible military threat to enemy maneuver and freedom to attack.

In an effects-based framework, effects fall into two broad categories: direct effects, or those immediate outcomes created by "blue" (friendly) actions, and indirect effects, higher-order effects created upon "red" (adversary) or "gray" (neutral) actors within the operational environment. The counterair framework, illustrated in Figure 3.1, shows typical "blue" actions taken to create effects in support of counterair operations.

The counterair framework describes a number of different tasks or missions, each of which is described below. Note that in many cases the distinctions between the categories may blur. For example, an attack on an enemy SAM site may be considered an attack operation or SEAD. The finer distinctions do not substantially change the way operations are conducted, but may help Airmen to understand the elements of OCA and DCA.

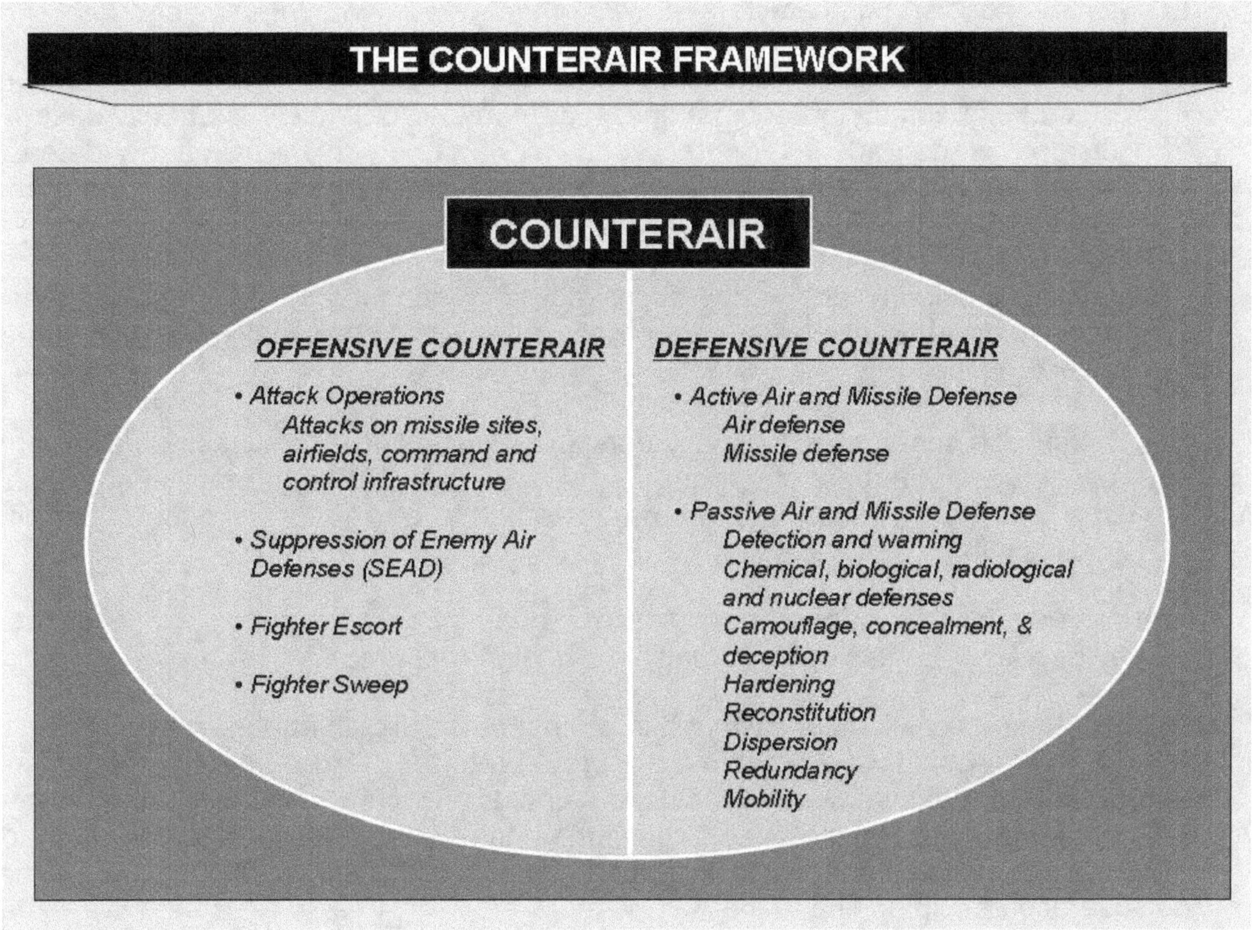

Figure 3.1. The Counterair Framework
(Based on Joint Publication 3-01)

Offensive Counterair

Different types of OCA operations are used to achieve specific counterair effects. Tasked units normally have decentralized execution authority and are given significant latitude in the detailed planning and coordination of the tasks.

⊙ **Attack operations.** Attack operations are intended to destroy, disrupt, or degrade counterair targets on the ground. These missions are directed against enemy air and missile threats, their C2, and their support infrastructure (e.g., airfields, launch sites, launchers, fuel, supplies, and runways). The main goal is to prevent enemy employment of air and missile assets.

⊙ **Suppression of enemy air defenses.** SEAD is an OCA mission designed to neutralize, destroy, or degrade enemy surface-based air defenses by destructive or disruptive means. SEAD requirements may vary according to mission requirements, system capabilities, and threat complexity. SEAD planners should coordinate with

ISR operators to ensure collection and exploitation opportunities are considered prior to destroying or disrupting emitters. SEAD operations fall into three categories:

✪✪ Area of responsibility (AOR)/joint operating area (JOA) air defense suppression: Operations conducted against specific enemy air defense systems to destroy, disrupt, or degrade their effectiveness. It targets high payoff air defense assets, resulting in the greatest degradation of the enemy's total system and enabling effective friendly operations.

✪✪ Localized suppression: Operations normally confined to geographical areas associated with specific ground targets or friendly transit routes, contributing to local air superiority.

✪✪ Opportune suppression: Usually unplanned, including aircrew self-defense and attack against targets of opportunity. The JFC or JFACC normally establishes specific ROE to permit airborne assets the ability to conduct opportune suppression.

✪ **Fighter sweep.** An offensive mission by fighter aircraft to seek out and destroy enemy aircraft or targets of opportunity in a designated area (JP 1-02).

✪ **Escort.** Escorts are aircraft assigned to protect other aircraft during a mission (JP 1-02). Escort missions are flown over enemy territory to target and engage enemy aircraft and air defense systems. Friendly aircraft en route to or from a target area may be assigned escort aircraft to protect them from enemy air-to-air and surface-to-air threats. Typically, escort to low-observable ("stealth") aircraft requires special consideration and planning at the AOC level.

Defensive Counterair

Several types of DCA tasks also help to provide a permissive environment for friendly air action.

✪ **Active air and missile defense**. Active defense is defensive action taken to destroy, nullify, or reduce the effectiveness of air and missile threats against friendly forces and assets. It consists of two broad categories:

✪✪ Air defense. Defensive measures designed to destroy attacking enemy manned or unmanned air vehicles in the atmosphere, or to nullify or reduce the effectiveness of such attack.

✪✪ Missile defense. Defensive measures designed to destroy attacking enemy missiles, or to nullify or reduce the effectiveness of such attack.

These two tasks are closely integrated to form essential DCA capabilities, but may involve different defensive weapon systems or TTP.

⊙ **Passive air and missile defense**. Passive defense includes all measures, other than active defense, taken to minimize the effectiveness of hostile air and missile threats against friendly forces and assets. It consists of several categories of activities. These are briefly summarized in the section on execution considerations for passive defense:

✪✪ Detection and warning.

✪✪ Chemical, biological, radiological, and nuclear (CBRN) defenses.

✪✪ Camouflage, concealment, and deception.

✪✪ Hardening.

✪✪ Reconstitution.

✪✪ Dispersion.

✪✪ Redundancy.

✪✪ Mobility.

✪✪ Electronic and infrared countermeasures.

✪✪ Low-observable (stealth) technology.

The list of potential counterair effects is endless and will vary from operation to operation. Nonetheless, there are certain considerations applicable to planning, executing, and assessing counterair effects, which are detailed in the following sections.

PLANNING CONSIDERATIONS

Counterair planning may be conducted at every echelon of command and across the range of military operations. Counterair planning should take into account the capabilities of all the Services, joint force components, and interagency and multinational partners. Counterair planning is conducted using the joint operation planning process for air. For details on this process, see AFDD 2, *Operations and Organization*, Chapter 6 and JP 3-30, *Command and Control for Joint Air Operations*. During JIPOE, planners should determine the adversary's active and passive counterair capabilities, as well as his intent to contest air control with those capabilities, if possible. This, in turn, should inform the JFACC's and JFC's decision-making efforts during mission analysis and course of action development.

Normally, **the JFACC's first priority should be to define—in both time and space—that level of air control needed to achieve the JFC's objectives**. Once defined, the JFACC should identify the current level of control in the air (parity, superiority, or supremacy) and what actions are required to reach the desired level of control. This determination will drive the priorities for AOC planners. AOC planners and the JFACC must inform the JFC as to which level of air control is realistically achievable given current capabilities and allocation of assets. When analyzing forces available, it is important to consider the capabilities of other joint force components and multinational partners.

Offensive Counterair

Space in which to maneuver in the air, unlike fighting on land or sea, is practically unlimited, and...any number of airplanes operating defensively would seldom stop a determined enemy from getting through. Therefore the airplane was, and is, essentially an instrument of attack, not defence...

...The only proper defence is offence.

—Air Vice-Marshal J. E. 'Johnnie' Johnson, Royal Air Force top scoring Allied fighter ace in the European Theater of Operations, World War II, with 38 victories

OCA may be the highest payoff air component mission when the enemy has the capability to significantly threaten friendly forces with air and missile assets. Given finite resources, the JFACC should judiciously allocate them in order to meet the JFC's objectives. Successful OCA results in greater freedom *from* attack, enabling increased freedom of action and freeing assets for other operations against the enemy. In other words, the initial investment in OCA operations to achieve the desired level of air control may pay significant dividends toward overall mission accomplishment. Determining which enemy capabilities hinder air control is fundamental to successful OCA operations. For instance, it may not be necessary to completely destroy a given capability, but only temporarily degrade it in order to achieve desired effects. The latter may require much less effort, thereby freeing up assets for other missions. This type of analysis may vary from one operation to another but often results in an effective set of target priorities and an efficient use of assets to achieve the desired effects.

Offensive Counterair Example

To gain control of the air, friendly forces must counter enemy airborne threats not only to assure full force protection, but also to enable full flexibility to conduct parallel operations across the operational environment. The flexibility of air power may tempt commanders to divert it to other tasks. The theater commander must correctly balance requirements; it is the role of the air component commander to articulate the crucial enabling role of air, space, and cyberspace superiority. Relaxing pressure on the enemy's air forces may allow them to gain air superiority with disastrous results. For example, Hitler's decision during World War II to divert the Luftwaffe from direct attack of the Royal Air Force (RAF) to the bombing of cities allowed the RAF breathing space it desperately needed to reconstitute and eventually win the Battle of Britain.

What the Luftwaffe failed to do was to destroy the fighter squadrons of the Royal Air Force, which were, indeed, stronger at the end of the battle than at the beginning.

—Air Chief Marshal Sir Hugh C.T. Dowding Fighter Command, Royal Air Force

The nature of airpower is such that offensive combat power can frequently be "massed" by *distributing* forces. In fact, the most effective OCA efforts may be achieved as part of a broader, parallel attack on the adversary as a system-of-systems. For instance, attacking electrical power and isolating national military leadership may aid the operation's overall OCA effort while also helping achieve other objectives. However, as with other operations, care must be taken not to dilute the OCA effort to the point where it is ineffective. Concentration of effort in the context of space and time will ensure that direct effects allowing access are balanced with indirect effects that degrade the overall enemy system over time. If the OCA effort is spread too thin, the JFACC risks losing the initiative and the benefits of airpower's offensive nature. When considering counterair assets available, it is important to give full consideration to the assets and capabilities of other components.

Planners should assume at a minimum that adversaries will have at least a rudimentary IADS, consisting of both active and passive defenses, even if they do not possess any significant offensive air potential. IADS range from coordinated fire from small-caliber antiaircraft artillery, man-portable air defense system (MANPADS) missiles and small arms fires (which may, nonetheless, employ sophisticated passive measures such as camouflage and concealment), to complex, integrated, and highly redundant systems such as the Israelis encountered in the 1973 Yom Kippur War and the US encountered in North Vietnam, Serbia, and Iraq during Operation SOUTHERN WATCH. In all cases, strategists and planners should develop means of neutralizing these systems, or negating their effectiveness, in order to create a permissive air environment at desired places and times. In the case of the more complex IADS, attacking the larger enemy system in parallel (versus concentrating on the IADS alone) will likely be more effective and may yield cascading failures within the IADS, as systems it relies upon also fail. Ironically, more rudimentary or "primitive" defense systems may be harder to defeat because they are more distributed and easily concealed (or otherwise protected), and may be rendered ineffective only by imposing operating restrictions on friendly forces (since such defense systems are typically short-ranged).

The following considerations are important for determining OCA targeting priorities and methods:

- ✪ **Threat.** The threat posed by specific enemy capabilities (aircraft, theater missiles, etc.) includes an assessment of the urgency or the need to counter that threat. A WMD-capable missile launcher would normally merit diversion of assets from a less immediate threat, such as a SAM site.

- ✪ **Direct effects.** First-order results of actions with no intervening effects between action and outcome. These are usually immediate, physical, and readily recognizable (e.g., weapon employment results). These are important in determining whether friendly tasks were accomplished. Planning for them must also consider such factors as collateral damage potential and rules of engagement restrictions.

- ✪ **Indirect effects.** Second, third, or higher-order effects created through intermediate effects or causal linkages following causal actions. These may be physical, psychological, functional, or systemic in nature. They may be created in a cumulative, cascading, sequential, or parallel manner. They are often delayed and typically are more difficult to recognize and assess than direct effects. Understanding these and the causal linkages between them may be vital for achieving objectives.

- ✪ **Forces available.** The forces available are assessed against the number, types, and priority of targets that can be attacked. Sufficient and capable forces should be provided to ensure the desired results are obtained.

- ✪ **Time available and time required.** Time constraints are integral to prioritization and planning. The time allowed to achieve the direct and indirect effects as well as the duration required of those effects will influence the number and type of forces required.

○ **Risk.** Risk calculation involves weighing the risk to friendly forces against expected gains from target attack. Risk calculation should also consider the risks entailed in *not* taking planned actions. Different objectives and circumstances drive different acceptable levels of risk.

○ **Measures and indicators.** These are the essential component parts of assessment; the means of evaluating progress toward creating effects and achieving objectives. They should be determined during planning. See the section on assessment, below, for greater detail.

The types of resources available to perform OCA tasks (listed under "execution," below) are only "tools" in a planner's "toolkit." Desired effects should drive planning efforts and there may be many ways to impose a particular effect. The means may be chosen based on a number of criteria, including desired higher-order indirect effects. For example, there are multiple ways to suppress a SAM site. One may simply jam its communications and radars if short term, local suppression is needed, or if resources needed to create the intended effects are not available. One may destroy or degrade the operations center that controls the site, forcing the enemy to autonomous operations that often present less of a threat to friendly forces. One may destroy the site outright if its autonomous operation represents a sufficient threat to friendly operations. Planners and commanders should choose means carefully in order to satisfy requirements relating to the timing and tempo of operations, the persistence of threats, and "opportunity costs" of using OCA assets for other purposes.

Planning for OCA usually takes place in the AOC as part of the joint operation planning process for air (see AFDD 2). In early stages of planning, the JFACC, along with the AOC's strategy and ISR divisions, will determine objectives, desired effects, and relative priorities. Planners in the strategy, combat plans, and ISR divisions will determine enemy systems, capabilities, and assets that can be used to contest air control. Combat plans and combat operations personnel will use this information to match desired effects to targets provided by the ISR division, and match targets with friendly forces to create tactical tasks. Planners should develop a prioritized target list before hostilities begin, continually updating it once the battle rhythm is established based on current intelligence and progress of the operation. Planners should also build procedures to handle higher priority re-taskings, such as diversions to strike JFC-designated time-sensitive targets (TSTs), which, for counterair, may be such targets as enemy ballistic missiles or the most modern "strategic" SAMs that represent significant threats to friendly air operations. Planners must be able to rapidly retask OCA missions in order to take appropriate action against TSTs and similar fleeting, emerging, or higher-priority OCA targets. For example, it may be necessary to pull a flight of aircraft off of attacking an enemy aircraft fuel facility to strike (or monitor) a probable ballistic missile launch site that is of higher priority to the JFACC and JFC. A frequently used best practice is to designate on-call aircraft with appropriate weapons loads to loiter, awaiting the call to strike a fleeting target, then striking a pre-planned OCA (or other) target if no call comes. Against fixed, often highly defended, targets deep within enemy territory, OCA planners should place great emphasis on detailed, accurate, and timely intelligence, target analysis, time-over-target deconfliction, active and passive defenses available to the enemy, and ROE. Mission planners at the unit level should study these thoroughly to avoid fratricide and mission interference, and enhance mission effectiveness.

The following considerations are important for OCA planning at the AOC and unit mission planning levels:

☼ **Enemy threat, location, and capabilities.** The enemy threat to air operations needs proper consideration in the planning, positioning, and timing of OCA mission details. Specific threats to the OCA effort (aircraft, missiles, AAA, electronic attack) may require substantial emphasis be placed on their disruption prior to striking intended targets.

☼ **Friendly C2 capabilities.** Theater C2 assets such as AWACS and JSTARS, are tasked by numerous units and agencies. As such, OCA planners should not assume that complete C2 capabilities will be available for every OCA mission. In all cases, C2 instructions should be carefully monitored, because this is the avenue through which higher-priority re-tasking will come.

☼ **Rules of engagement.** ROE (and related special instructions [SPINS]) found in tasking orders, as well as rules for use of force, often used in situations such as homeland defense and civil support missions) may critically affect how missions are performed. All levels, from the JFACC down to individual aircrews, should understand the ROE that apply to the accomplishment of their missions.

☼ **Weaponeering.** Assigning the correct weapons and platforms to a specific target set is a critical job. Accurate weaponeering increases the chances of achieving desired effects.

☼ **Deconfliction.** The sheer number of airborne assets—manned, unmanned, and ballistic—demands that planners deconflict to protect friendly forces from unnecessary risk.

☼ **Environmental conditions.** The significance of environmental conditions on counterair cannot be overstated. Weather can limit sensor or seeker sensitivity and ultimately limit the planner's munitions selection. Likewise, varying terrain can be a challenge to pilots or offer refuge to an adversary. Terrain will often limit munitions selection. Planners should address the need for sufficient counterair assets to offset the loss of capability and desired effects due to environmental factors.

☼ **Distance, timing, and refueling.** OCA and DCA air assets typically require refueling support for sustained presence. Refueling coordination requires constant management by planners, and details need to be stated in ATO SPINS. See Chapter 1 and AFDD 2-6 for more detail on refueling considerations.

Defensive Counterair

While OCA seeks to affect enemy counterair systems close to their source, DCA seeks to affect those same systems closer to their intended targets. In some cases, DCA may also be the only allowed means of countering air and missile threats due to constraints imposed by the political situation. Effective OCA greatly reduces the DCA requirement, freeing assets for more offensive operations, but some degree of DCA is normally necessary in every operation. DCA operations defend friendly lines of communication, protect friendly forces and assets by denying the enemy the freedom to carry out offensive attacks from the air, and provide a secure area from which all elements of the joint force can operate effectively. DCA operations can be conducted in conjunction with or independent of OCA operations and generally fall into one of two categories: Active or passive defense.

Just as in OCA operations, DCA planners prioritize which assets and capabilities to defend. Planners at all levels identify enemy targets and capabilities to defend against, while matching available forces against the threat. They use many of the same OCA planning considerations. Planners determine which mission-critical assets and capabilities to protect, which will vary from operation to operation.

The future threats facing the joint force commander will be even more diverse, more lethal and more difficult to detect and kill than we face today. And they are going to include manned and unmanned, stealthy and non-stealthy vehicles, ballistic missiles and cruise missiles. Faced with this diverse threat array, the JFC will need an integrated offensive and defensive counterair approach to destroy or neutralize enemy aircraft and missiles.

—General Ronald Fogleman, CSAF, 1994-1997

Active Air Defense

Active air defense is direct defensive action taken to destroy, nullify, or reduce the effectiveness of hostile air and missile threats against friendly forces and assets (JP 1-02). Active air defense operations are conducted using a mix of weapon and sensor systems, supported by secure and highly responsive C2 systems, to find, fix track, target, and destroy or reduce the effectiveness of hostile airborne threats. These operations attempt to neutralize or degrade the effectiveness of enemy attacks and protect friendly forces and interests through the **direct employment** of weapons systems. Active air defense targets include any airborne threat that negatively impacts friendly operations.

Integrated employment of air-to-air and surface-to-air defense systems through coordinated detection, identification, engagement, and assessment of enemy forces is necessary to defeat enemy attacks and protect friendly forces. Planners should keep in mind the complexities of airspace control in a DCA environment. Airspace control in an active air defense environment is extremely difficult and becoming more complicated with the proliferation of UAS. Rapid, reliable, and secure means of identification are critical to the survival of friendly aircraft and to facilitate an effective defense against enemy air and missile attacks.

The efficient execution of air defense operations requires the ability to quickly detect a potential air defense threat, identify it, target and track it, and attack it. DCA engagements may occur inside friendly airspace, requiring careful deconfliction between friendly assets, such as fighters in the DCA role and friendly SAMs. An agile ISR capability is essential to provide continuous surveillance and reporting of real time and near-real time target track data. To maximize damage to the enemy force, the engagement process is continuous throughout the threat's approach, entry into, and departure from the friendly operational area. Target track production is a sequential process that begins with the surveillance function.

Near-real time surveillance and threat analysis depends on the ability to fuse all-source sensor data (ground, air, sea, and space-based sensors) into an accurate theater attack assessment. As a track is detected, it is identified and labeled; this information is then disseminated as rapidly as possible. The track data provided should be sufficiently detailed and timely to permit the C2 system to evaluate the track, determine the significance of the threat, and designate air defense forces for interception. The optimum employment of air defense weapon systems involves the earliest possible discrimination of friend from foe to maximize beyond-visual-range engagement. **To prevent fratricide, great caution should be exercised when employing autonomous CID in DCA operations.**

If no IADS is established, procedural means should be used to permit the safe passage of friendly aircraft while still allowing for the use of air defense weapons (fighter engagement zones, missile engagement zones, and joint engagement zones). Since many DCA assets are owned by different Services and coalition partners, standardized integration, coordination, and airspace control procedures are required to enable or enhance the capabilities of the various systems. Finally, ROE should remain simple, giving air defense systems the flexibility to operate beyond the constraints of procedural control measures. For a more detailed discussion of air defense operations, see AFDD 2-1.7, *Airspace Control in the Combat Zone*.

Passive Air Defense

Unlike active air defense measures, passive air defense does not involve the employment of lethal weapons. Rather, these measures improve the survivability of friendly forces by reducing the potential effects of enemy attacks. Passive air defense measures are designed to provide protection for friendly forces and assets by complicating the enemy's identification, surveillance, and targeting processes and by countering the enemy's planned effects.

The first step of passive air defense is to hide valuable assets from the enemy or to encourage him to attack decoys. Like active air defense measures, a thorough passive defense should include layered defense in depth. Passive measures can work concurrently to achieve this goal. These measures include camouflage, concealment, and deception; hardening; reconstitution; dispersal; electronic and infrared countermeasures; and low observable (LO) or stealth technologies. Passive air defenses are often an additional means of defense should active air defense efforts fail.

EXECUTION CONSIDERATIONS

During the ongoing battle rhythm, weapon systems are matched to specific targets to carry out tasks. The types of air assets employed and the target sets affected differ between OCA and DCA.

Offensive Counterair

The effectiveness of OCA operations depends on the availability of certain resources. System capabilities are influenced by the situation, threats, weather, and available intelligence. The following are some of the resources used to conduct OCA:

- **Aircraft.** Fighter and bomber aircraft provide the bulk of the weapon systems for OCA operations. Other types of aircraft and weapon systems are often critical enablers of counterair operations (e.g., electronic attack, electronic protection, and air refueling aircraft).

- **Missiles.** These weapons include surface-to-surface, air-to-surface, and air-to-air missiles, as well as air-, land-, and sea-launched cruise missiles. Many of these weapons have long ranges and some have very quick reaction times. These weapon systems can eliminate or reduce the risk of harm to friendly forces by destroying enemy systems in the air and on the ground.

- **ISR systems.** ISR systems and resources may be used in counterair operations to provide intelligence, surveillance, reconnaissance, deception, and other effects against enemy forces and air defense systems. These activities include the use of airborne, space-borne, and ground (e.g., human intelligence) assets.

- **Unmanned aircraft systems.** UAS may be used in counterair operations to provide ISR, deception, jamming, harassment, or destruction of enemy forces and air defense systems. These systems may be preprogrammed or remotely piloted. They provide valuable intelligence to friendly forces and may now be used to attack some targets either too dangerous or risky for manned aircraft or where manned aircraft are not present or available to respond. They may also be used to help provide persistent air presence over enemy forces in situations where this may have important psychological effects upon an adversary (as part of OCA or other operations) if synergistically tasked to help provide persistent presence over adversary forces.

✪ **Special operations forces (SOF).** SOF can conduct direct action missions, special reconnaissance, and provide terminal guidance for attacks against valuable enemy targets. Planners in the AOC coordinate with the special operations liaison element to coordinate the use of special operations assets in support of the counterair mission.

✪ **C2 Systems.** These systems enhance OCA operations by providing early warning, intelligence, identification, and targeting data, as well as C2 of friendly forces.

✪ **Information operations (IO) and cyberspace operations.** IO and cyberspace operations can greatly enhance joint operations, in some cases reducing the demand for sorties. Many OCA targets such as C2, theater missiles and support infrastructure, and airfields/operating bases can be affected by various IO and cyber techniques (such as network attack operations). Some of these techniques are able to affect targets that may be inaccessible by other means.

✪ **Electronic warfare** assets are frequently the most vital to any effective operation to suppress enemy C2, IADS, and other significant military use of the electromagnetic spectrum. See AFDD 2-5.1, *Electronic Warfare Operations*, for detailed discussion of all aspects of electronic warfare.

✪ **Surface fire support.** Artillery and naval surface fire support may be employed in OCA operations. With the proper coordination, this may be a very effective way to destroy enemy targets while minimizing risk to friendly forces.

✪ **Surface Forces.** The ability to destroy, damage, secure, and occupy key OCA and DCA systems (such as SAM sites), as well as the lethality of supporting surface fires, can achieve vital counterair effects. Israel used this synergy to attain air superiority during the 1973 Yom Kippur War. After the Normandy breakout in World War II, advancing Allied troops, denied the enemy airbases while acquiring those for friendly OCA and counterland efforts.

OCA target sets are those which directly or indirectly challenge control of the air. Ideally, OCA concentrates on degrading the capabilities of these targets as close to their source as possible (e.g., aircraft on airfields, theater missiles and SAMs in storage). Otherwise, OCA missions seek and attack targets whenever and wherever they can be found: on the ground, in the air, or at sea. The following are representative OCA target sets, and do not reflect the full spectrum of potential OCA employment:

✪ **Electronic warfare capabilities.** Left unhindered, enemy electronic warfare (EW) operations could have devastating effects on friendly C2 systems. Early and persistent efforts should be aimed at defeating enemy EW capabilities.

✪ **Airfields and operating bases.** Damaging runways or taxiways may prevent use of an airfield for short periods. Destruction of support facilities—hangars, shelters, maintenance facilities, fuels—degrades the enemy's ability to generate aircraft sorties. CBRN weapons and materials may be stored at these locations to be loaded onto aircraft.

○ **Aircraft.** This category includes enemy fixed-wing, rotary-wing, and unmanned aircraft. In most situations, aircraft on the ground are the most lucrative targets for OCA operations. Precision weapons with penetration capabilities may be combined with timely intelligence to destroy aircraft on the ground regardless of enemy sheltering or hardening efforts.

○ **Missiles and support infrastructure.** "Missiles" refers to ballistic, cruise, and air-to-surface vehicles. Missiles may pose a significant threat to friendly forces. These missiles may possess conventional as well as CBRN capabilities. OCA operations seek to destroy or disable these missiles before they are launched. Destruction of missiles, launch platforms, support facilities, and infrastructure greatly limits effective missile attacks against friendly forces or territory.

○ **C2 systems.** C2 systems are critical to the effective employment of forces and integration of IADS and should be given a high priority during OCA targeting. Intelligence-gathering, warning, and control systems, including ground-controlled intercept, early warning, acquisition, and other sensors, together with their supporting facilities, form integral parts of an IADS. Destruction or nonlethal disruption of such systems may substantially reduce the enemy's capability to detect, react, and bring forces to bear against friendly forces.

○ **Air defense systems.** Disruption or destruction of enemy IADS and the personnel who control, maintain, and operate them may render those systems ineffective against friendly forces.

Defensive Counterair

No single defensive system is impregnable. Therefore, the most effective use of defensive assets is a defense-in-depth approach, or the "layering" of mutually supporting defensive positions designed to absorb and progressively weaken enemy attacks. When working in unison, the limitations and advantages of some assets are balanced by the limitations and advantages of other assets. Some of the primary assets used in conducting active air defense missions are discussed below:

○ **Fighter aircraft.** Fighter aircraft are used to accomplish any of the air defense missions, with the objective of intercepting and destroying hostile missiles and aircraft before they can reach their intended targets. These aircraft use combat air patrols to ensure rapid reaction to enemy attacks and may be positioned well ahead of forces being protected.

○ **Armed helicopters.** Armed helicopters may conduct limited DCA operations when required. C2 relationships with these armed helicopters performing DCA missions will be determined by the JFC. Armed helicopters can engage targets such as enemy helicopters, battlefield air defenses, and other targets within their combat range.

☼ **High value airborne assets (HVAA)**. HVAA are assets that are in high demand, but in limited supply. For example, ISR assets provide surveillance, early warning and identification capability. Other assets, such as the EA-6B aircraft, can provide electronic attack and protection, while tankers are required to extend the range and/or sortie duration of other airborne assets.

☼ **Surface-to-air weapons.** Surface-to-air weapons effectiveness requires a highly reliable link with air operations and a reliable identification process. This process must preclude engagement of friendly aircraft and unnecessary expenditure of valuable resources. All available surface-to-air defense assets in the theater of operations are incorporated into the overall DCA plan and are subject to the integrated procedures, ROE, and weapons control measures directed by the AADC. The AADC should be granted the necessary authority to deconflict and control engagements and to exercise real time battle management when required.

Active defense missions. With respect to DCA, it is better to speak in terms of types of missions assigned rather than types of targets, since these will be fleeting and will differ from situation to situation. Units employed to create air defense effects usually have decentralized execution authority and the necessary latitude in the detailed planning and coordination of assigned DCA tasks. The following types of missions are most closely associated with active air defense operations:

☼ **Area Defense**. Area defense missions are conducted for the defense of a broad area using a combination of weapon systems. There can be more localized applications of area defense when friendly assets are dispersed over a large geographical area with defined threat boundaries.

☼ **Point Defense**. Point defense missions are conducted for the protection of a limited area, normally in defense of the vital elements of friendly forces and installations.

☼ **HVAA Protection**. HVAA protection uses fighter aircraft to protect critical airborne theater assets.

☼ **Self-Defense**. Self-defense is conducted by friendly forces to defend themselves against direct attack or threat of attack through the use of organic weapons and systems. Inherent to all ROE and weapon control procedures is the right of self-defense.

Passive defense entails the following actions:

☼ **Detection and warning systems**. Timely detection and warning of air and missile threats provide maximum reaction time for friendly forces to seek shelter or take other appropriate action against enemy attacks. Missile warning is especially vital to friendly forces considering the compressed timelines for detection and warning of missiles.

- ✪ **Chemical, biological, radiological, and nuclear defensive elements**. CBRN elements are made up of contamination avoidance, protection, and contamination control. Contamination avoidance measures include covering critical assets, remaining inside facilities during attacks, detecting and identifying contaminated areas, and avoiding those areas. Protection includes such things as collective protection facilities and individual protective equipment. Contamination control is standard disease prevention and control measures, contaminated waste management, and decontamination procedures. For further details on CBRN defense, see AFDD 2-1.8, *Counter-Chemical, Biological, Radiological, and Nuclear Operations*.

- ✪ **Hardening**. Valuable assets and their shelters are hardened to protect against hostile attacks. Hardening actions are usually accomplished during peacetime, but may continue throughout operations.

- ✪ **Reconstitution**. This capability provides for the rapid repair of damage resulting from enemy attacks and the return of damaged units to a desired level of combat readiness. Reconstitution includes the ability to repair valuable assets such as airfields, communications, warning and surveillance systems, and to restore essential services such as power, water, and fuel supplies.

- ✪ **Redundancy**. Duplication of critical capabilities keeps vital systems functioning even when critical nodes are destroyed or damaged. Redundancy includes dual, contingency, or back-up capabilities which can assume primary mission functions, in whole or in part, upon failure or degradation of the primary system.

- ✪ **Dispersal**. Dispersal complicates the enemy's ability to locate and target friendly assets by spreading them out and bringing them together in concentration only at the time and place of our choosing. Combined with mobility and deception, dispersal increases uncertainty as to whether a location is occupied or will remain occupied. It forces the enemy to search more locations, requiring more resources and time.

- ✪ **Mobility**. Mobility is the capability to easily move from one location to another and is facilitated by keeping a small footprint. Frequent movement of units, inside the enemy's decision cycle, can be of critical importance. Mobility reduces vulnerability and increases survivability of friendly assets by complicating enemy surveillance, reconnaissance, and targeting.

- ✪ **Electronic and Infrared Countermeasures.** Electronic and infrared countermeasures are measures possessed by individual aircraft or systems that typically attempt to defeat enemy weapons during their track or guidance phase. Onboard systems are often a prerequisite for aircraft to conduct missions.

○ **Stealth and LO technology**. Stealth and LO technologies are those measures, normally designed into a weapon system, which attempt to hide or minimize its presence during mission execution, or reduce the vulnerability to enemy threat systems.

What do we defend?
...think like the enemy:

From an Airman's perspective, these priorities are derived from an assessment of what capabilities are required to conduct successful *offensive* operations.

○ **Air Operations Command and Control:** The AOC and its associated lines of communication to its air units, including satellite links, secure net connectivity, secure telephone and land lines, or any other critical node necessary for air operations.

○ **Aircraft Generation and Support:** Fuel supply lines, maintenance facilities, runways, etc., used for aircraft generation are critical single point failure nodes for air operations.

○ **HVAA Protection:** HVAA are critical force enablers and multipliers. AWACS, RIVET JOINT, JSTARS, certain ISR platforms, and in some cases tankers are subject to protection as HVAA.

○ **Intratheater Command and Control:** The CRC and other intra-theater ground forces command and control lines should be protected.

○ **Fielded Forces and Supply Lines:** Fielded forces, which may have some internal air defense capability, and their supply lines are critical to offensive and defensive ground operations. This includes intratheater airlift air defense as well.

ASSESSMENT

Assessment encompasses all efforts to evaluate effects and gauge progress toward accomplishment of tasks, effects, and objectives. It also helps evaluate requirements for future action, helping answer two questions: "Are we doing things right?" and "Are we doing the right things?" In an effects-based construct, it is not possible to think about actions and their effects without considering how creation of those effects should be measured. Assessment applies as much to the conduct of counterair operations as to any other air, space, or cyberspace function. In fact, assessment may be more tangible and immediate in the case of counterair operations: if an enemy site shoots at friendly aircraft, it may warrant immediate dynamic targeting or at least inclusion on the next tasking cycle's list for deliberate targeting. Assessment is performed by personnel in the strategy, ISR, and combat operations divisions in the AOC.

Measures and indicators

Measures are empirical observations used to evaluate progress of an operation. Indicators are things that can be inferred from existing evidence to indicate progress. These may be either quantitative or qualitative in nature. All of these must be determined and linked to friendly tasks and desired effects during planning. The types of measures and indicators used in assessment are described below.

At all levels of assessment, planners should choose criteria that describe or establish when actions have been accomplished, desired effects have been created, and objectives have been achieved. There are three distinct types of measures and indicators:

✪ **Measures of performance**: Objective or quantitative measures assigned to the actions of a task and against which a task's accomplishment, in operations or missions terms, is assessed. At the tactical level, measures of performance (MOPs) are generally related to weapons effects on individual targets. Operational level tasks and MOPs are typically broader and system-based (e.g., the number of SAM sites neutralized versus number of SAM sites operational).

✪ **Measures of effectiveness (MOEs) and success indicators**: Quantitative or qualitative measures assigned to an intended effect (direct or indirect), against which the effect's creation is directly assessed. Some of these may be direct forms of measurement, such as first-hand observation of an early warning radar's destruction; some may be more circumstantial or indirect, such as signals intelligence reports of no emissions from the radar site. Success indicators evaluate progress toward objectives and MOEs measure progress toward effects.

Assessing the degree of friendly air control is challenging. The inherent characteristics of airpower—speed, range and flexibility—apply to enemy air and missile threats as well, which makes assessment of enemy actions and intent more difficult. As previously stated, the JFACC's first priority is to determine the level of air control needed to achieve the JFC's objectives. All subsequent planning and assessment is based on this determination. A thorough understanding of the enemy system and its components should logically drive the development of friendly objectives, effects and tasks. The key to effective assessment is to develop measures and indicators *at the same time* as the objectives, effects and tasks they measure—not after the fact. Measures and indicators should be either directly observable, or something that can be reliably inferred from other data.

Task performance is typically the easiest to measure. At the tactical level MOPs feed combat assessment: Was the mission flown? Were weapons released as intended? Did they create the weapons effects anticipated? Within the AOC, the ISR division's analysis, correlation, and fusion cell uses these tactical data to determine the status of enemy air systems (operational status of airfields, enemy sorties flown, SAM sites destroyed) and feeds this data to the operational assessment team (OAT) within the strategy division. Operational level tasks (e.g., neutralize enemy SAM systems) are also measured by MOPs and provide a big-picture report to the JFACC on task performance.

Measuring effects in the counterair fight may seem daunting, but the very purpose of counterair operations provides some guidance: counterair is conducted to ensure freedom to maneuver, freedom to attack, and freedom from attack. The effects associated with counterair will necessarily be related to these three items. It is possible to measure, directly, the number of successful friendly and enemy air attacks as well as the number of missions (or friendly operations) affected by enemy air activity. The desired effects will also be based on the level of air control required (as determined by the JFACC). Regardless of which effects are desired, or how they are measured, one important point must be understood: task performance and effect performance must be measured (and reported) independently.

Measuring task and effect performance separately provides the clearest picture of progress towards achieving the objective. The expected outcome of these measures and indicators is a rough alignment between task, effect, and objective performance. Since tasks were designed to create effects—and desired effects lead to the achievement of objectives—this makes sense. When the levels of performance in task, effect and objective do *not* align it may have a profound effect on future actions in the OCA or DCA effort.

For example, if a large number of enemy airfields are assessed as degraded due to runway damage (high task performance), but the enemy continues to generate a large number of sorties (low effect performance) then the OCA plan needs to be examined. How does the enemy continue to generate sorties? Are they rapidly repairing the runways? Have they relocated to other airfields or highway strips? Perhaps airfield runways are not a critical node of the enemy system after all—and the focus should shift to targeting fuel or munitions storage. These are questions that never would have revealed themselves if task performance was the sole determinant of success in the objective.

Even more revealing is a high level of effect performance, accompanied by low task performance. To use the example above, suppose that only a few enemy airfields have been targeted, but the enemy air force does not generate a single sortie. The enemy is clearly capable of flying, but for some reason (as yet unknown) does not fly. Future actions, in this case, will depend on the amount of risk the JFACC is willing to accept. If the acceptable level of risk is low—enemy airfields will continue to be attacked until the enemy's potential sortie count is very low. In effect: the task performance will "catch up" to the effect performance and the risk of attack from enemy aircraft will be very low. Conversely, if the JFACC is willing to accept a higher risk (or, if the enemy subsequently buries his aircraft in the sand) efforts may shift away from airfields to other components of the enemy IADS—or to different objectives entirely.

OCA and DCA performance may be measured separately, or they may be combined depending on the course of action selected. In many cases, desired effects for air control are applicable to both DCA and OCA. For example: OCA efforts to shut down enemy sortie production will necessarily have a positive impact on the DCA effort since fewer enemy aircraft will be available to challenge friendly air defenses. Conversely, successful enemy air attacks on friendly airfields (due to unsuccessful DCA efforts) will have a negative impact on friendly sortie generation—affecting both DCA and OCA (and other mission types as well.)

Effective assessment is a key feature of the effects-based approach to operations, and if done correctly should generate as many questions as answers. Warfare is a clash between living, thinking systems which react to one another in often unexpected ways. By measuring friendly actions (tasks) and changes in the enemy system (effects) separately, critical review of actions and effects becomes possible. The questions: why are my actions not producing results? Why is the enemy behaving in this manner? What changes should be made to the plan – and why? These are exactly the questions and answers the JFACC needs to effectively prosecute the JFC's objectives.

The future battle on the ground will be preceded by battle in the air. This will determine which of the contestants has to suffer operational and tactical disadvantages and be forced throughout the battle into adopting compromise solutions.

—General Erwin Rommel

At the very heart of warfare lies doctrine…

SUGGESTED READINGS

Air Force Publications
(Note: All AFDDs are available at **https://www.doctrine.af.mil**, AFTTP(I)s at **https://wwwmil.alsa.mil/index.html**)

AFDD 1, *Air Force Basic Doctrine*
AFDD 2, *Operations and Organization*
AFDD 2-1, *Air Warfare*
AFDD 2-1.7, *Airspace Control in the Combat Zone*
AFDD 2-1.8, *Counter-Chemical, Biological, Radiological, and Nuclear Operations*
AFDD 2-1.9, *Targeting*
AFDD 2-5.1, *Electronic Warfare Operations*
AFDD 2-6, *Air Mobility Operations*
AFDD 2-8, *Command and Control*
AFDD 2-9, *Intelligence, Surveillance, and Reconnaissance Operations*
AFTTP 3-1, Vol. 26, *Theater Air Control System*
AFTTP(I) 3-2.17, *Theater Air Ground System*
AFTTP(I) 3-3.21, *Integrated Air Defense System*

Joint Publications

JP 1-02, *Department of Defense Dictionary of Military Terms*
JP 3-0, *Joint Operations*
JP 3-01, *Countering Air and Missile Threats*
JP 3-09.3, *Joint Tactics, Techniques, and Procedures for Close Air Support*
JP 3-30, *Command and Control for Joint Air Operations*
JP 3-40, *Joint Doctrine for Combating Weapons of Mass Destruction*
JP 3-52, *Joint Doctrine for Airspace Control in a Combat Zone*

Other Publications

Cooling, Benjamin F., *Case Studies in the Achievement of Air Superiority* (Washington DC, Center for Air Force History). 1994.

Cordesman, Anthony H., *The Lessons of Afghanistan: War Fighting, Intelligence, and Force Transformation* (Washington DC, Center for Strategic and International Studies), 2002.

Dempster, Derek and Derek Wood, *The Narrow Margin: The Battle of Britain and the Rise of Airpower, 1930-40* (Washington DC, Smithsonian Institution Press). 1990.

Finney, Robert T., *History of the Air Corps Tactical School, 1920-1940,* USAF Historical Study 100 (Maxwell AFB, AL, Air University Press). 1995.

Futrell, Robert Frank, *Ideas, Concepts, Doctrine: Basic Thinking in the United States Air*

Force, Vol I (Maxwell AFB, AL, Air University Press). 1989.

Gulf War Air Power Survey, Vol II (Washington DC, US Government Printing Office). 1993.

Hallion, Dr. Richard P., *Control of the Air: the Enduring Requirement* (Washington DC, Air Force History and Museums Program). 1999.

Hudson, James J., *Hostile Skies: A Combat History of the American Air Service in World War I* (Syracuse, NY, Syracuse University Press). 1968.

Lambeth, Benjamin S., *Air Power Against Terror: America's Conduct of Operation ENDURING FREEDOM* (Santa Monica CA, RAND Corporation), 2005.

Mann, Edward C. Col. USAF, *Thunder and Lightning* (Maxwell AFB, AL, Air University Press). 1995.

McFarland, Stephen and Wesley Phillips Newton, *To Command the Sky: The Battle for Air Superiority over Germany, 1942-44* (Washington DC, Smithsonian Institution Press).1991.

Mets, David R., "To Kill a Stalking Bird," *Air Power Journal* (Maxwell AFB AL, Air University Press), Fall 1998.

Momyer, William M., *Airpower in Three Wars* (Maxwell AFB AL, Air University Press, reprint edition), April 2003.

Reynolds, Richard T. Col. USAF, *Heart of the Storm* (Maxwell AFB, AL, Air University Press). January 1995.

Thompson, Wayne, To *Hanoi and Back: The U.S. Air Force and North Vietnam, 1966-1973* (Smithsonian Institution Press). 2000.

Warden, John A. III, Col (Ret.), *The Air Campaign: Planning for Combat* (Washington DC, National Defense University Press). 1998.

Weyland, O.P., "The Air Campaign in Korea," Air University Quarterly Review, Vol 6 (Maxwell AFB AL, Air University Press). Fall 1953.

GLOSSARY

Abbreviations and Acronyms

AAA	antiaircraft artillery
AADC	area air defense commander
AADP	area air defense plan
ACA	airspace control authority
ACE	airborne command element
ACM	airspace control measure
ACO	airspace control order
ACP	airspace control plan
AFDD	Air Force doctrine document
AFTTP(I)	Air Force tactics, techniques, and procedures (interservice)
AOB	air order of battle
AOC	air and space operations center
AOR	area of responsibility
ASOC	air support operations center
ATO	air tasking order
AWACS	airborne warning and control system
C2	command and control
CAOC	combined air operations center (JP 1-02) combined air and space operations center {USAF}
CBRN	chemical, biological, radiological, and nuclear
CFACC	combined force air component commander (JP 1-02) combined force air and space component commander {USAF}
CID	combat identification
COMAFFOR	commander, Air Force forces
CRC	control and reporting center
COP	common operational picture
CSAF	Chief of Staff, United States Air Force
CSAR	combat search and rescue
DCA	defensive counterair
EW	electronic warfare
HVAA	high value airborne asset
IADS	integrated air defense system
IO	information operations
ISR	intelligence, surveillance, and reconnaissance

JAOC	joint air and space operations center
JFACC	joint force air component commander (JP 1-02), joint force air and space component commander {USAF}
JFC	joint force commander
JIPOE	joint intelligence preparation of the operational environment
JOA	joint operations area
JP	joint publication
JSTARS	joint surveillance target attack radar system
LO	low observable
MANPADS	man-portable air defense system
MOE	measure of effectiveness
MOP	measure of performance
OAT	operational assessment team
OCA	offensive counterair
OEF	Operation ENDURING FREEDOM
OPCON	operational control
RADC	regional air defense commander
RAF	Royal Air Force (UK)
ROE	rules of engagement
SADC	sector air defense commander
SAM	surface-to-air missile
SEAD	suppression of enemy air defenses
SOF	special operations forces
SPINS	special instructions
TACS	theater air control system
TAGS	theater air-ground system
TST	time-sensitive target
TTP	tactics, techniques, and procedures
UAS	unmanned aircraft system
USAF	United States Air Force
WMD	weapons of mass destruction

Definitions

active air defense. Direct defensive action taken to destroy, nullify, or reduce the effectiveness of hostile air and missile threats against friendly forces and assets. It includes the use of aircraft, air defense weapons, electronic warfare, and other available weapons. Also called **air defense.** (JP 1-02)

air control. Air control describes a level of influence in the air domain relative to that of an adversary, and is categorized as parity, superiority, or supremacy. (AFDD 2-1.1)

air defense. Defensive measures designed to destroy attacking enemy aircraft or missiles in the atmosphere, or to nullify or reduce the effectiveness of such attack. See also **active air defense; aerospace defense; passive air defense.** (JP 1-02) [*Defensive measures designed to destroy attacking enemy manned or unmanned air vehicles in the atmosphere, or to nullify or reduce the effectiveness of such attack.*] (AFDD 2-1.1) {Italicized definition in brackets applies only to the Air Force and is offered for clarity}

air domain. The area, beginning at the Earth's surface, where the atmosphere has a major effect on the movement, maneuver, and employment of joint forces. (AFDD 2-1.1)

airspace control authority. The commander designated to assume overall responsibility for the operation of the airspace control system in the airspace control area. Also called **ACA.** (JP 1-02)

airspace control in the combat zone. A process used to increase combat effectiveness by promoting the safe, efficient, and flexible use of airspace. Airspace control is provided in order to prevent fratricide, enhance air defense operations, and permit greater flexibility of operations. Airspace control does not infringe on the authority vested in commanders to approve, disapprove, or deny combat operations. Also called **combat airspace control; airspace control.** (JP 1-02)

air parity. A condition in the air battle in which one force does not have air superiority over others. (AFDD 2-1.1)

air superiority. That degree of dominance in the air battle of one force over another which permits the conduct of operations by the former and its related land, sea, and air forces at a given time and place without prohibitive interference by the opposing force. (JP 1-02) [*That degree of dominance in the air battle of one force over another that permits the conduct of operations by the former and its related land, sea, air, and space forces at a given time and place without prohibitive interference by the opposing force.*] (AFDD 2-1.1) {Italicized definition in brackets applies only to the Air Force and is offered for clarity}

air supremacy. That degree of air superiority wherein the opposing air force is incapable of effective interference. (JP 1-02) [*That degree of dominance in the air battle* *of one force over another that permits the conduct of operations by the former and its related land, sea, air, and space forces at a given time and place without effective interference by the opposing force.*] (AFDD 2-1.1) {Italicized definition in brackets applies only to the Air Force and is offered for clarity}

area air defense commander. Within a unified command, subordinate unified command, or joint task force, the commander assigns overall responsibility for air defense to a single commander. Normally, this is the component commander with the preponderance of air defense capability and the command, control, and communications capability to plan and execute integrated air defense operations. Representation from the other components involved is provided, as appropriate, to the area air defense commander's headquarters. Also called **AADC.** (JP 1-02)

combat identification. The process of attaining an accurate characterization of detected objects to the extent that high confidence and timely application of military options and weapons resources can occur. Also called **CID.** (JP 1-02)

control. Authority which may be less than full command exercised by a commander over part of the activities of subordinate or other organizations. (JP 1-02)

counterair. A mission that integrates offensive and defensive operations to attain and maintain a desired degree of air superiority. Counterair missions are designed to destroy or negate enemy aircraft and missiles, both before and after launch. See also **air superiority; defensive counterair; offensive counterair.** (JP 1-02)

cyberspace. A global domain within the information environment consisting of the interdependent networks of information technology infrastructures, including the internet, telecommunications networks, computer systems, and embedded processors and controllers. (AFDD 2-11).

defensive counterair. All defensive measures designed to detect, identify, intercept, and destroy or negate enemy forces attempting to attack or penetrate the friendly air environment. Also called **DCA.** See also **counterair; offensive counterair.** (JP 1-02) *[Defensive counterair operations are synonymous with air defense operations. Defensive counterair encompasses both active and passive measures and is normally conducted near or over friendly territory and generally reacts to the initiative of enemy forces.]* (AFDD 2-1.1) {Italicized definition in brackets applies only to the Air Force and is offered for clarity}

direct effect. First-order result of an action with no intervening effect between action and outcome. Usually immediate, physical, and readily recognizable (e.g., weapons employment results). (AFDD 2)

effect. 1. The physical or behavioral state of a system that results from an action, a set of actions, or another effect. 2. The result, outcome, or consequence of an action. 3. A change to a condition, behavior, or degree of freedom. (JP 3-0)

effects-based approach to operations. An approach in which operations are designed, planned, executed, and assessed in order to influence or change system behavior to achieve desired outcomes. (AFDD 2)

electronic warfare. Any military action involving the use of electromagnetic and directed energy to control the electromagnetic spectrum or to attack the enemy. Also called **EW.** (JP 1-02)

fighter sweep. An offensive mission by fighter aircraft to seek out and destroy enemy aircraft or targets of opportunity in a designated area. (JP 1-02)

high-payoff target. A target whose loss to the enemy will significantly contribute to the success of the friendly course of action. High-payoff targets are those high value targets that must be acquired and successfully attacked for the success of the friendly commander's mission. (JP 1-02)

indirect effect. A second, third, or nth-order effect created through an intermediate effect or causal linkage following a causal action. It may be physical, psychological, functional, or systemic in nature. It may be created in a cumulative, cascading, sequential, or parallel manner. An indirect effect is often delayed and typically is more difficult to recognize and assess than a direct effect. (AFDD 2)

information operations. The integrated employment of the core capabilities of electronic warfare, computer network operations, psychological operations, military deception, and operations security, in concert with specified supporting and related capabilities, to influence, disrupt, corrupt or usurp adversarial human and automated decision making while protecting our own. Also called **IO.** (JP 1-02) *[Information operations are the integrated employment of the core capabilities of influence operations, electronic warfare operations, network warfare operations, in concert with specified integrated control enablers, to influence, disrupt, corrupt or usurp adversarial human and automated decision making while protecting our own.]* (AFDD 2-5) {Italicized definition in brackets applies only to the Air Force and is offered for clarity.}

joint force air component commander. The commander within a unified command, subordinate unified command, or joint task force responsible to the establishing commander for making recommendations on the proper employment of assigned, attached, and/or made available for tasking air forces; planning and coordinating air operations; or accomplishing such operational missions as may be assigned. The joint force air component commander is given the authority necessary to accomplish missions and tasks assigned by the establishing commander. Also called **JFACC.** See also **joint force commander.** (JP 1-02) *[The joint force air and space component commander (JFACC) uses the joint air and space operations center to command and control the integrated air and space effort to meet the joint force commander's objectives. This title emphasizes the Air Force position that air power and space power together create effects that cannot be achieved through air or space power alone.]* [AFDD 2] {Words in brackets apply only to the Air Force and are offered for clarity.}

missile defense. Defensive measures designed to destroy attacking enemy missiles, or to nullify or reduce the effectiveness of such attack. (JP 1-02)

missiles (and support infrastructure). Ballistic missiles, cruise missiles, and air-to-surface missiles pose a significant threat to friendly forces. These missiles may possess conventional as well as chemical, biological, radiological, and nuclear (CBRN) capabilities. OCA operations destroy or disable these missiles before they are launched. Destruction of known missiles, launch platforms, support facilities, and infrastructure greatly limits effective missile attacks against friendly forces. (AFDD 2-1.1)

offensive counterair. Offensive operations to destroy, disrupt, or neutralize enemy aircraft, missiles, launch platforms, and their supporting structures and systems both before and after launch, but as close to their source as possible. Offensive counterair operations range throughout enemy territory and are generally conducted at the initiative of friendly forces. These operations include attack operations, fighter sweep, escort, and suppression of enemy air defenses. Also called **OCA.** (JP 1-02) [*Offensive operations aimed at destroying, disrupting, or degrading enemy threats that affect the air domain.*] (AFDD 2-1.1) {Words in brackets apply only to the Air Force and are offered for clarity.}

operational control. Transferable command authority that may be exercised by commanders at any echelon at or below the level of combatant command. Operational control is inherent in combatant command (command authority). Operational control may be delegated and is the authority to perform those functions of command over subordinate forces involving organizing and employing commands and forces, assigning tasks, designating objectives, and giving authoritative direction necessary to accomplish the mission. Operational control includes authoritative direction over all aspects of military operations and joint training necessary to accomplish missions assigned to the command. Operational control should be exercised through the commanders of subordinate organizations. Normally this authority is exercised through subordinate joint force commanders and Service and/or functional component commanders. Operational control normally provides full authority to organize commands and forces and to employ those forces as the commander in operational control considers necessary to accomplish assigned missions. Operational control does not, in and of itself, include authoritative direction for logistics or matters of administration, discipline, internal organization, or unit training. Also called **OPCON.** (JP 1-02)

operational environment. A composite of the conditions, circumstances, and influences that affect the employment of capabilities and bear on the decisions of the commander. (JP 1-02)

parallel attack. Offensive military action that strikes a wide array of targets in a short period of time in order to cause maximum shock and dislocation effects across an entire enemy system. (AFDD 2)

passive air defense. All measures, other than active air defense, taken to minimize the effectiveness of hostile air action. These measures include camouflage, concealment, deception, dispersion, reconstitution, redundancy, detection and warning systems, and the use of protective construction. See also **air defense.** (JP 1-02)

rules for the use of force. Directives issued to guide United States forces on the use of force during various operations. These directives may take the form of execute orders, deployment orders, memoranda of agreement, or plans. (JP 1-02).

rules of engagement. Directives issued by competent military authority that delineate the circumstances and limitations under which United States forces will initiate and/or continue combat engagement with other forces encountered. Also called ROE.   (JP 1-02).

suppression of enemy air defenses. Activity that neutralizes, destroys, or temporarily degrades surface-based enemy air defenses by destructive and/or disruptive means. Also called **SEAD.**   (JP 1-02)

unmanned aircraft. An aircraft or balloon that does not carry a human operator and is capable of flight under remote control or autonomous programming. Also called **UA**. (JP 1-02)

unmanned aircraft system. That system, whose components include the necessary equipment, network, and personnel to control an unmanned aircraft. Also called **UAS**. (JP 1-02)